Labyrinth

Rita Signorelli-Pappas

Labyrinth

Rita Signorelli-Pappas

SERVING HOUSE BOOKS

Labyrinth

Copyright © Rita Signorelli-Pappas

All rights reserved.

No part of this book may be used or reproduced in any manner whatsoever without the prior written permission of the copyright holder except for brief quotations in critical articles or reviews.

ISBN: 978-1-947175-15-0

Library of Congress Control Number: 2019942240

Cover photograph by Rita Signorelli-Pappas

Serving House Books logo by Barry Lereng Wilmont

Published by Serving House Books

Copenhagen, Denmark and Florham Park, NJ

www.servinghousebooks.com

Member of The Independent Book Publishers Association

First Serving House Books Edition 2019

For René Steinke, Katie Trumpener,
Mollie Sandock, and Jim Brokaw

And for the memory of Richard Maxwell

Acknowledgments

Grateful acknowledgment is made to the editors of the following magazines in which these poems, sometimes in slightly different form, first appeared:

The American Voice: "Winged Victory"
College English: "Memory of Florence"
Notre Dame Review: "Annunciation," "Psyche and Cupid"
Poet Lore: "Tea with Franny Glass," "Questions for Rainer Maria Rilke"
Prairie Schooner: "Artemisia"
The South Carolina Review: "Epilogue for Baucis and Philemon"
Southern Humanities Review: "Snapshot"
Southern Poetry Review: "House of Refuge," "Persephone to Demeter"
Valparaiso Poetry Review: "Requiem"

Contents

1. LABYRINTH

Tulips   11
Artemisia   12
Labyrinth   13
The Salt Chronicles   15
Anafiotika   19
House of Refuge   21
Winged Victory   22
Epilogue for Baucis and Philemon   23
In a Wintry Season   24

2. SNOW: A MEMOIR

Snow: A Memoir   27
Abstractions of the Libido   31
Sand Dollar   33
Orpheus   34
Hawk   36
The Pedigree   37
Mink Farm   38
Annunciation   39
Forty-eight Hours in Venice   40
After the Stigmata   41

3. WAITING FOR THE BUDDHA

Tea with Franny Glass   45
Waiting for the Buddha   47
Manhattan, 1967   48
The Cemetery at Sutri   49
The Lesson of Luo Ping   50
Requiem   51
Testimony   52
Butterflies   53
Portrait of Ivan   54
Snapshot   55

4. WHAT THE HORSES KNOW

Something like Contentment   59
Images for a Tapestry   60
Persephone to Demeter   62
Desire   64
Toward the Solstice   65
Psyche and Cupid   66
Memory of Florence   68
Questions about Rainer Maria Rilke   69
Leda   70
The Years with Bertran de Born   72
You Wake as the Charioteer of Delphi   73
A Studio in November   74
What the Horses Know   75

1. LABYRINTH

Tulips

Down the well of soul darkness
their crimson petals prepare to fall
like shards of painted glass.

For days they stood impassive
but now their translucence quickens
into a ghostly human tableau.

With the precision of mimes
they carve their consummate gestures
of rapture and despair from the April light.
They lean out sinuously in open space
articulating every twist
as if it were a law of passion.
Each day I pause to watch
while everything I know hesitates
before the ease of their abandon—
they keep on reaching
for the higher air as if they
could brush up against the sky

or light every candle in my heart
to signify that love is deeper than
what I have imagined for myself.

Then like an exclamation their petals drop
and the rhythm of my blood breaks
into the runaway beat of a star.

Artemisia

I want to enter your death
and let you walk me through it
from the moment it first
gazed at you and smiled
with a slow wink,

I want to know what
enchanted words it whispered
the instant you leaned forward to listen
with such a wild concentration
your whole body forgot to breathe.

I want to leave behind my own body
like a weaver abandoning a broken loom
and find the door of that room where
your misty gaze has muffled the edge
of every window, every book.

I want to watch the way
the shuttle of your imagination
moves like a butterfly across the garden
interlooping the moonlit blossoms
with filaments of shining haze.

And when I have seen each image
I want to dance every rhythm
of your dark, delicate death
taking it gently in my arms
like an attentive cavalier.

Labyrinth

The sky over the labyrinth
the silver script unrolling
into clouds that dissolve
into a trail of hoofprints
wandering like a path
through satin halls the walls

woven with the broken
threads of secrets never told
will you ever stop vanishing
into yourself will you dare
to raise or lower your eyes
if you imagine the way out

it will only disappear the years
will keep closing behind you
the backlight will never clear
you can neither sleep nor wake
in the endlessly unfolding blue
each moment of your life

plunging ahead of you into
what you cannot hear or see
the ground below your feet
cartwheeling into sky the blood
in your veins a tilted pulse-lit
dream twirling forward

without you was there
ever a time when your mind
did not lean or whirl when
the narrow corridors of your life
suddenly stopped swaying

The Salt Chronicles

The lifelong griefs dissolved
into an echo of ringing crystal,
the sweet, sharp motes of voices singing
through empty caverns of salt.
The mind roamed an ocean hermitage
hidden in hollows of silence and light.

Capri, Island of the Sirens

Manta rays glide, folding and unfolding.
The body enters and is entered.
A brutal humming drifts from the shore
to browse the shallows of his thigh.
An acrid moon scatters the waves
with the sequined smoke of salt.

Jerusalem, The Garden Tomb

To love and be loved by what was wounded.
Desire for the pierced wrist and brow.
To hear his voice and feel a warmth at her
    shoulder.
To reach for what was near but could not be
    touched.
To follow and follow the melting paths of foam
with the sting of seawater in her mouth.

The Road from Sodom

Was it the cryptic ash of snow
or the spectral mists of rain
crowding her veins with the tender
mouths and gestures of the city?
She turned and the pain pearled her body
into a glowing monument of brine.

Florence, San Marco Convent

The fragrant heat of loaves rising.
The angels floating waist-deep in clouds.
His cowl sewn shut, they would lower him
and he would feel the stone walls loosen,
the soul preserved by what was gilded
with flakes of sugared and salted gold.

Venice, Pietá Conservatory

Thick or thin, the resined strings are not a dream
but the vibrations through which he drifts
into a room full of orphaned girls playing violins,
his hands rising and plunging like giddy swallows
as the chords come spinning over his head
like waves flinging salty pebbles on the sand.

Kyoto, Studio near the Gion Shrine

Wind blows the orchard leaves with coolness.
The husband and wife work all night
on tattered mats behind a torn screen.
The stars tick. The moments crystallize
into pure white morsels of the infinite.
The trees fill with fingertips, tongues.

St. Petersburg, Nevsky Prospect

Above the neck scarf, a pair of avid eyes.
The young man strolling the boulevard
carries holy, bitter salt in his pocket
so that moonlight will blunt the knife's edge
and crown his heart with ashes,
so that his life will endure and disappear.

New York, Studio in the Bowery

Black earth and shadow: the precisions of pain.
Minerals coagulate to dissolve.
Flame narrows over a bowl filled with salt and oil.
Waking or sleeping, she sees herself
woven in the reticulations of a hanging web,
tangled and knotted, shining and undone.

To think without words. To feel the momentum
of the clouds grow and blossom into light.
To breathe the astringent smoke of memory
like a ceremonial incense. Or to sail alone
in a worn glass boat dreaming and singing
the stern, cleansing rhapsodies of salt.

Anafiotika

*In the mid-nineteenth century, a village was built
on the Acropolis hillside by migrants from the
island of Anafi.*

A half-remembered twilight.
Stone and the fragrance of pine.
Were we in Athens or a deserted island village?

An unease as quiet as the cats watching us
behind shutters along the winding street
and high above, the caryatids dreaming in mid-air.

A sheep once grazed under the olive tree.
Now there was only an empty chair.
The masons of Anafi came hoping to build a
palace.

The blank Cycladic moon was hidden
in corridors of cloud as we paused on the path
taking us deeper inside a labyrinth

where hanging wash snapped in the breeze
like distant sails riding the Aegean wind
while settlers on a ship waited, listening.

There was something like belief
still spiriting through the cottages,
a fleeting caravan of whiteness

filing toward the promised dark
that would change our lives
into what was incised and infinite.

House of Refuge

The veined violet marble moon
that waits beyond the willow tree
remembers the night it saved you
from the wind's strong embrace.
It led you here through the esplanade
into this breathing house of refuge.
Lie down silently under raveled boughs
snaking into a lattice of human hair.
Come early when the tree glows
white with moon-fire. Sleep and see
with closed eyes the loyal shadow
that never lost sight of you,
you the fugitive, passing through
the suburbs of this weary life
with your circus of tender mysteries,
your magic grotto of ghostly bones
that can set root in any silence.
Climb the magnetic hills of dreams
until the blue and winnowing air
loosens the slow, shrill song
of your long desolation, until
the space encircling your body
is a radiance so cold
imagination cannot warm it.

Winged Victory

The Louvre

I caught a glimpse of you
as I climbed the stairs—
winged girl without a gaze,
your aura torn away the moment
they wrenched your body from the mast,
the moment of your final gesture when
your bold spirit dissolved, the moment
when you stopped looking back at us,
when you lost your desire for touch.

And now you roar into the silence
like a bonfire over ice
through your wild two thousand years
of tearless voiceless exile, you whose
song resounds above the gardens of the park,
beyond the triumphal arch, beyond the mute
forward rush of sunflowers in Burgundy.

Epilogue for Baucis and Philemon

If I had known it was our last conversation,
if I had seen your head lower to the incoming fog,
if I had listened without bitterness to the words
you broke like twigs from the silence of hemlock forests,
if I had noticed your thoughts starting to thin
into dark solitary buds, if I had pulled
you up from the chair to your feet
and embraced your stiff swaying body on that night
you stood alone bruised and fragrant as a cinnamon tree,
if there had been time to reminisce like Baucis and Philemon
and hold a transparency of our life together to the light,
then perhaps I would not have entered this white
apocalypse of leaves and perhaps I would not be telling you
how the gray bark has hooded me like a cloak
of linen cloud or how these winter suns burn
like ceremonial fires with cold clear vanishing flames.

In a Wintry Season

In the poem I was a phoenix in a bamboo grove
but outside the day was cold and endless.
On a shelf inside our house I placed a small
Chinese vase between your photograph and mine.

The hours unroll inked in monochrome.
Thoughts link and interweave like plum tree branches.
Our dead emerge like shadows from the snow
to guard us with the force of breath.

We make gestures of devotion,
you lifting your hands over a piano keyboard,
I conjuring images from the smoke of burning pine.
Words condense between us through clouds and mist.

The vase is painted with a scene of two figures
lying in the shade of a pavilion by a lotus pond.
The moss encrusts our roof, and desire recedes
as lightly as the moments of a dark season.

2. SNOW: A MEMOIR

Snow: A Memoir

1.

There were shadows flickering in the eye.
Images in the mind that tapped on stone.
A scarf floated out behind me shredded and white.
There were no gestures to muffle the feral wind.
No garden waiting down the path of night.

2.

I was drifting in the spray
of a waterfall frozen into place.
I wasn't realistic, was I?
At the end there was nothing left
to bequeath but a craving for touch.

3.

Dreams attacked me in stages of snow.
Mists unraveled: a cryptic grief.
A light more than star rose somewhere in me.
The impulse to embrace left echoes underground
like a charred, leafless tree.

4.

There was an obsession with words.
They filed through the wilderness
like the ghosts of Chinese warriors.
I was avid, wasn't I? Underneath each
pulsed syllable was the heat of memory.

5.

And in the blue, separate world of the heart
blood continued to move. *I was judgmental,
wasn't I? I wore costumes of grievance
like ritual robes.* In the chest: music.
In the mind: the whirling presence of snow.

6.

People entered and left. Shadows shook their heads.
Sighed. *I was naïve, wasn't I?*
There were certain tests of sensibility.
The impulse to practice a craft.
It was a life of insufficient laughter.

7.

There was death and its aftermath.
Beyond blackout the siren call back.
Then the return—hypnotic and clear.
Days shorn like hair. Prayer books torn.
The colossus of love lying like ruins in a museum.

8.

There were weeks of roaming forests
with red omnivores. *I was fearful, wasn't I?*
At five I never slept—the el train kept me awake.
Then the eyes close. The boundless light
of childhood goes rushing away.

9.

There was the ruse of trust.
The perpetual impulse toward thought.
Moments of lust. In the mute forest
a spectral self composed sentences of snow.
There were gates closing. Transparencies of intent.

10.

Flurries came at dawn or at dusk.
The words twirled and spun.
There was an aura of impenetrable beauty.
A perfection that could not be touched.
I was jealous, wasn't I?

11.

There were failures in kindness.
Tapestries of the self stitched
with filaments of cloud. Something
was written beneath the whiteness.
Daylight. The silence of snow.

12.

Life stood like a plague doctor
hooded and masked. *I was alone, wasn't I?*
But the pain kept drifting into music.
The flakes fell syllable by syllable.
Voices were whispering beyond the snow.

Abstractions of the Libido

Flame is the greeting
of fingertips, the inescapable
return in an astral orbit.
There are certain flora and fauna,
the images of petals, leaves.
There is the circling bee of thought.

The body lies on a bamboo couch
while the walls drift off into waves
painted in the colors of shadow.

A cobra bite brings drowsiness,
the snow sketches silhouettes
of plum blossoms in ash.

Tie a long twig to your wrist
and the soul's white ink will splash
into the calligraphy of stars.

You measure the emptiness,
enter an equation for pleasure
balanced on an axis of pain.

The brutal agitations
of a flute come spinning
from the Eleusian air.

There is a pair of torches,
a head sprinkled with water and oil,
the taste of barley in the mouth.

A crane is flying in the twilight.
Statues of the immortals line the road.
Moments unscroll into a chanting mist.

And what you feel
in the seclusion of a hermitage
is not tenderness or prayer.

A sudden wave breaks—
every atom of your body dissolves
in a frisson of blue-green light.

The landscape tilts and shifts
at the inflection point on a curve
charted in clouds, wingbeats, tides.

Sand Dollar

Deathless shell of an emptied longing,
once you lay buried like an afterthought
in a mermaid's cave or you stood
edgewise on the seafloor, your
incisions sifting salt and sand
with a holy wounded tenderness.

So long as passion is the pure
isolate gesture of the soul
your contours will wear
the imprint of an orchid or a star.

You will undulate and glow
in the twilight of subterranean
tombs, rolling on like a manta ray
in your quiet sleigh of pearl,
living on in your private exile
to expire and bloom again
in a pale medallion of bone-light
left by the receding tide.

You lie in the patterned silence
stony and light to the touch,
fixed in your way of knowing
how to leave the world.

Orpheus

Snake's eye thinning to a slit.
Did he deserve such goodness?
Why should the gods love him now?

His music woke the night,
raised the veil from her face,
froze the venom drop at the center of the soul.

She would always cleave to him
and he would never leave her glance
as she drew him endlessly to her,

as the supple dream of her body,
coiling and uncoiling, polishing itself,
floated in his gaze.

So he kept walking toward the light
dreaming of her still while the
menace of reverie enfolded him,

a rainbow rippling across his skin,
while impatience closed over him
an umbrella of liquid silk.

Suddenly she was invisible in his mind.
She no longer walked behind him—
there was only the chiming

of a flute inside his ear,
then a tremor at his waist,
the blue embrace of satin tentacles.

Desire scattered him to a cloud of ink
while the words of his song came back to him
Passion was too strong a god

and the sensate air whitened
when he turned around to see
what his arms once held weaving into mist

and the Furies kept weeping
as he saw the pattern of his loss
rewoven at the loom, yes this was

the death he drew deep down into
the cold black earth of his body
where it took root, budded, and bloomed

but by then he had reached the light,
he lived in time's pauses and twists,
the evasions of an alluring flute,

and passion had long become
the lonely, endured music of distance,
darkness ripening into song.

Hawk

      To hear the cry of a hawk
            to feel the weight of soul
balanced
                        on a cliff's edge
    glide of the blade
        slicing through eternity
                hiss of an unknown god
     abrading the air
              a pair
of implacable eyes
             the wings
      flexed for darkness or light
the urge to descend emptiness
                to exist beyond weather and time
      the slow terrible tenderness
             spread out like a quilt
                    over trees wind
clouds

The Pedigree

I used to envy the pedigrees of well-born friends.
For decades my mother waited, then finally told me
how each morning she would wake to the sound
of the door opening and her father entering her bed.

He had carved a machete that he used to guard their
    house.
He had murdered a man once and deserted the Italian
    army.

Years later he sent me a copy of *The Divine Comedy*
covered in torn shelf paper with the words of Ulysses
marked: *You were not meant to live as beasts.*

Now I no longer think about the pedigrees of friends
but the silence of Darwin in the Galapagos.
I remember the unease in my grandfather's face,
the darting eyes and deliberate way of rolling back
his upper lip to expose the gums and teeth, now I can
    feel
in that sly giggle the chill of the forest shriek.

Mink Farm

You came back into the trees
with the force of a sudden vow
avid as a cellist meditating
before exploding into wildness.

You came from a house of confused
intensity the leathery whirring
of straps being swung what stirred
in your mind was something

swirled into sanctity the ardor
of a wave growing and breaking
flowing all the way back into itself
toward a primal craving to know.

You came with a child's reprieve of time
before the cosmos could sweep you away
or hold you back from racing into the trees
to gaze at a row of tin roofs set low

but though you crouched to concentrate
there was nothing else to see
except the evil in life
cryptic and unknown.

Annunciation

The whir of a wing-beat
through mild morning light, the sense
of white fragrant mist and then
the blurred strands of a form thickening—
not quite a woman nor man—it was
something that could not be touched yet
she felt the plunge coming toward her,
how every particle in her body yielded
the moment she recoiled from that
weightless radiance, for there was something
crystallizing the instant it dissolved—
there was the astonishment of ambush
in blue air rustling like a satin robe
tumbling over her head, the distracted
silhouette of her own arm extending
as she began to breathe the sweet smoky
syllables of words like a drift of incense,
the swaying gossamers clinging to her skin,
for now behind closed lids she saw
what would be as it was said—
there were the clear chords of a lute—
and what had she ever known except
these transparent threads of music rising
like wind gathering up the leaves
to weave them into circles and circles of light.

Forty-Eight Hours in Venice

I remember the first day in Venice   Carpaccio's courtesans and saints

     the first night at our hotel   a way station for moody gondoliers

         church lights flickering like candle flame on the water

a *traghetto* chugging by   the furtive footsteps of pedestrians

at breakfast the next morning   a man asked his wife   *hey are we having fun yet*

we listened without words   all night I had taken you into my body

     and a quiet wonder had settled over us

         like a refined mist from the Renaissance

After the Stigmata

The body elongating into shadow
her feet suddenly beautiful the ankles
starred with deep rosettes she could
feel the whirlwinds swirling
at her knees her hands woven
in a crimson latticework of snow

She was descending into the core
of her body she was entering
the salvation of silence and pain
she was moving past the boundaries
of her own skin now that
these wounds had healed her

She looked at the sky and saw
the existence of everything
all that a wound could recall
broke over her mind heart soul
what was scarred split open
the lips of the rupture spoke

3. WAITING FOR THE BUDDHA

Tea with Franny Glass

She was wearing such
odd steel-rimmed spectacles
and her hair had gone so gray
that I hardly recognized her
in the tearoom by the Spanish Steps.
I tried hard not to stare, remembering
she'd had a touch of neurosis in her youth.
Then I noticed her voice had lost
its quaver, she kept twisting
her bracelet and breaking into a smile.
Her appetite had improved as well,
she devoured all the scones
and asked for more. She welcomed
the opportunity to reminisce—
said Zooey had left the ashram
and was in Venezuela now, his
letters said papayas tasted sweeter
on the other side of the road.
He had changed much less than she, he
was still so handsome, he could still
talk circles around her, he still took
those long four-hour baths.
Les and Bessie had passed away.
Buddy had killed himself, of course.
Boo Boo ran a health spa in the Himalayas.
When I mentioned Seymour's name, she
changed the subject to her five children:
not one—thank God—was suicidal.
As we left the tearoom, she suddenly
shook my sleeve and whispered some instructions.

Then she entered a waiting cloud
and levitated high into the sky.
I stayed below but took
her final words to heart—
gave up thinking so I could follow
the Way of the One.

Waiting for the Buddha

I never knew how to speak to the Buddha,
I let the teachings in his books harden
into a perfection of circles and squares.
I never entered a sacred grove because the beauty
would bring such dizziness and my body would
feel so heavy I would have to let one arm
dangle like a monk flying in the wind.
With my eyes closed I could still imagine
my body floating like a monument down a river,
I could hear demons gathering in the field
chanting their cruel mantras, I could see them
waving their raffia baskets stuck with quills.
But I learned to subdue them with
poultices of light and though I never
spun a prayer wheel like a crazed pilgrim
I sat quietly on the branch of a tree
chewing and spitting pomegranate seeds
which was how I wandered the maze of loneliness.
So I did not bow to statues or do prostrations on a path,
I did not circle the monastery a hundred times a day
and at night I hardly noticed the petals of stars
chipping above me like plaster rosettes.
With my eyes closed, I was crouching in a meadow
like some small furred shadow of delight,
I was leading a caravan of lions, tigers, and deer.
We were headed for an abandoned grotto,
we were waiting for the Buddha
with webbed fingers and crystal eyes
to explode from his niche of cinnabar
and take us traveling like dragons into clouds.

Manhattan, 1967

Autumn and the leaves not yet dead.

We were walking to a restaurant
my imagination painted red,
your arms just brushing my shoulder
my hand barely touching your sleeve.

You'll like the Cafè Brittany,
you said and winked so lightly
I heard hoof-taps on the pavement.

Joy so pure that for an instant
it illuminated the veins of leaves.
Your voice so quiet it slipped over me
like the shadow of an old longing.

Autumn and the future not yet dead
and the silhouette of a red façade
beckoning us far into the twilight.

The Cemetery at Sutri

We drifted through the cemetery delirious
hearing only the voices that greeted us
from another life, we could hardly bear

the gazes of photographs watching us
from above the graves. There were no
fragments of statues, no bronze reliefs,

only the quiet breathing of moths asleep
inside their shells for the dead kept coming
nearer, their needs kept whispering in the air.

Their eyes flashed suddenly before us
like the spread of a peacock's tail.
They grew indolent consuming our reveries

and took liberties with our lives because
they knew our secrets, they stood there smiling
in the shadows so we could listen to our past.

Slowly we filled with their wonder as the walls
of our solitude whitened and the moments
composed themselves into gestures of stone.

The Lesson of Luo Ping

Since I cannot think like Luo Ping
I watch the walls of my room
tier into galleries of pearl.
Since I cannot brush oil on silk
I press my fingers against my lips
to ignite the Buddha's holy fire.

I want to carve the image of my heart
on the highest beam in Snow Hall.
I want to sit on a rootwood stool
and cruise the lonely cliffs
of my mind like a wild crane
while winds cleave the clouds.

That's why a crowd of hungry ghosts
keeps floating from the plum leaves
to strum a tune on my skeleton ribs.
That's why they call to me even
through the branches of my dreams.

All night I roam the open field
outside the temple of a banyon tree.
I clasp my hands behind my back
and the sacred grove fills with light
so the stars will know my feelings.

Requiem

The metronome ticks, the distant shadows
of caribou drift over snow and thoughts come
easily at twilight when beekeepers' ghosts
move through the empty orchard.

There is a rhythm to dream like the lost
breathing of the ancient parables, there is
a pulse to time in the scattered palpitations
of the stars as they travel their own solitude.

The imagination never sleeps as you do now,
the clouds will not stop racing through the heart
so rest forever in the holy footprint
of the Buddha while your meditations glide

far out over the sea and your soul unwinds
in syllables of foam flashing from the waves
and a blue sail slowly rises into the air
each time the night boat comes near.

        For Richard Maxwell

Testimony

When the master died I became
a monk of cloud and water
leaving my hut along the mountain path
only to beg or play with children.

I was called fool, seer, renegade
depending on the color of the leaves
And slowly my life separated
into the transparencies of poems.

I listen closely when the birds speak.
I see images and imagine words.
There is no cure for this loneliness,
No end to gathering such blossoms.

Butterflies

As I stepped through the mesh of flickering light
what greeted me was something more than air,
something giddy and blue faintly rinsing my eyes,
a sprinkled sliding like wind beginning in the trees,
there were butterflies suddenly everywhere filling
my mind with bold quicksilver flashes of ease,
they mastered me so swiftly it seemed I had always
lived in the random glimmer of their exactitudes
and that I could finally breathe with the freedom
of my lost buoyancy for already something like
eternity was retracing me in filaments of silk,
now all I wanted was this life suspended
in quivering petals of mist and my hands
floated as if I were spelling syllables
in the breeze, I felt the willow branches
shiver like waved dissolving wands,
perhaps I would muse and sway forever
on a tendril of grass yet something was
spicing the air with rue and thyme,
there was a spirit moving in the pulsation
of wings, there was a mind shifting
into dream, the darkness was breaking
in the cold night deserts of sorrow.

Portrait of Ivan

Like Ariel he was isolate and gleeful.
Like a pharaoh he would always lift his chin.
He could be cryptic and oracular.
Sometimes he walked like an antelope.

His madcap laughter came reeling over us
in sudden giddy waves and would send
our desolate work days spinning
into pinwheels streaming color and light.

He had the gusto of Vivaldi or Keats—
stood high-waisted, one bony-fingered
hand on hip, and strode triumphantly
straight through and past our lives.

He knew something more than we—
the savor of his own mortality—sitting alone
in his sunroom, he would smile when moths
began to flicker on the other side of the garden.

Snapshot

For Lena Signorelli
1924 – 1955

Today I unpacked
a vacation snapshot
of you as a teenager
astride a donkey
in Taormina.

I had lived
for forty years
without your picture.

But now I notice
your bare ankles
and straight shoulders,
the scorch marks
on the petals
of your orchid corsage.

Now you gaze back at me
from the mirror
with a face waxed blind
as an apple.

All night I dream you
back in Sicily,
hear your donkey's
high, weak laughter
rising through the palms.

4. WHAT THE HORSES KNOW

Something Like Contentment

I'll keep my eye on the black roof of a red barn
in the painting by Matisse.

I'll feel myself fall when the bridge
of the violin tilts and the strings snap.

No loneliness is as pure as the buildings
from the train window that morning in Bologna.

Some moments spike in you like fever.
Some kinds of fear bring the soul into balance

the way swallows flying over rooftops
plunge and right themselves in mid-air.

There is a kind of love that comes back to stare
through the feral tableau of a dream.

There is a kind of sorrow that lifts the sheet
over your head singing and brings you peace.

Images for a Tapestry

Swallows dive through the bell tower.
You wake in a swoon of pear blossoms.
Footsteps click on cobblestones, voices rise.

There is a strange high-pitched gaiety in the air
as the fortune teller sighs and begins to speak.

You light candle after candle but do not pray.
Your thoughts ride the penumbra of a smoking wick.

It seemed his death was the end of all goodness.
Caged in a sickroom, his mind paced and roamed.

Stone faces regard you from a great height.
The day smells faintly of clover and lime.
The blood stream chimes like an eternal carillon.

Quiet. Enigmatic. His eyes an infinity of blue.
His intense need to enter a painting on the wall.

John Cowper Powys. The cabinet of teas.
The garden's mysteries overgrown and wild.

He lay in bed, his rib broken—he continued to write.

It seemed the house was an edifice of leaves,
his life the source of all goodness
when night chalked a black cross on the door.

So you touched the stillness of his shoulders.
in a rendezvous that was
the underside of your contentment.

The moment when his chest stopped moving.
The moment the strains of the carillon ceased.

And now the clear agitation of glass ringing.
The pears ripening as the incense burns.

There is the sensation of breath.

>   For Katie Trumpener

Persephone to Demeter

With a cold, cut pomegranate
he rubbed the rim of a wine glass
that he slowly handed me.
And my breath broke like
a linen sheet ripped by wind.

But I knew I was going back to you
and remembered the tender way
you washed my arms with lemon sugar
to make them smooth—I felt my eyelids
thicken and close as they had when
the sea of narcissus folded me
in a bath of smoke.

The lavender burns all night, reminding me
of the tall, fragrant grass beside your door.
I want peace, warmth, and light, I want
escape from this huge drifting darkness,
I want to be in your cool white house
with its jewelled blue dome.

For eight months he will live
in the slit drum of his silence,
his kindness wounding me wherever I go.

I will grow used to the face that you wear
of a woman who has waited alone
at the stony waysides of strange lands,
a woman whose shoulders I will kiss
under autumn's yellow leaves.

Life has taken us, Mother,
beyond surrender and revolt.
With the veins of slaves
we fill pitchers and pour the clear water
that changes before our eyes
to our own bright, bitter blood.

Desire

Desire, my sweet companion, the torch
I hold against the wind, how can I ever
give you up? I would have to hide my face

under a cape of white and purple crocus,
forswear the scorched earth like Persephone
to find another way to breathe.

And as for my hands I would have
to use them to free myself
from the grip of my own longing

yet the sap keeps traveling, the leaves
are sifting light, a thick smoke lulls me
with reveries of balsam and fireweed.

There is a perfume spreading in the air,
drifting like a waxed wispy buzz,
there is a yearning breeze that follows me

when I walk the dream of your underworld,
there is a music in the woods impossible to
ignore as a finger on the lips, so desire,

my sweet companion, unclasp me slowly
like a glowing strand of pearls, inscribe me
deep in the windless caves of the dark.

Toward the Solstice

As I step into the rosy twilight
a fox crossing the road turns toward me
and vanishes into the trees.

It moves without confusion or awe
like the snake in my hall calmly
turning around to look back at me.

Or like Thoreau in his boat when he stopped
playing the flute and turned his face
toward a bright crescent moon.

The metaphors of grief subside
into an after-ring of snow
for there is warmth in the solstice

The sweetness of peace in the blood
a fox catching the soft scent of leaves
in a windless echoless December

Psyche and Cupid

Only when she laid her freshly bathed
white body on the corded bed and felt
the cool rustle of satin sheets, only the
strange sweet companionship of those voices
the instant she stepped over the threshold
of this empty mansion, only the ghostly chair
drawn back for her at that long banquet table
where no one sat but her, only the distant
whir of swallow wings in the blue filmy air,
the sudden odd flicker of candles lit by
an unseen hand, she was alone, only she had
felt his mysterious presence there with her
all afternoon and only now as she stretched out
on the green silk blankets and lifted her arms
high over her head, only now did she find her startled
hand stroking the air of a man and beyond hair
the stiff shock of linen wings, so this was finally he,
no monster after all but the husband she had
waited for, she heard his deep voice
murmuring in her ear while she gazed into
the dusk, these hushed smiling sounds drifting
from an invisible mouth and now she felt
a hand cupping her breasts and then
another hand stroking her cheek so gently,
her husband at last, and she let him caress her
all night, oh she abandoned herself
to that rolling waltz through life, through
death, the dance slower and slower now,
outside the soft shadows of morning splashed

among trees, outside the masses of hydrangeas
swaying, the darkness curved and narrowed
into a glowing shaft of light.

Memory of Florence

Fog slipped through the corridors
of that dreaming city
like some kept woman
craving a little sleep.

Only then did the moon's
oil lamp pass into smoke
while the squares seemed empty
of every voice, every gesture.

When torches suddenly flared
along the Old Palace roof
we ran out to the balcony
to hear the Liberation songs.

At dawn your mouth brushed
the edge of my body
like a deer browsing
low branches of pine.

Questions about Rainer Maria Rilke

Why was his middle name Maria?
How many letters did he write
to rich, beautiful women
begging them not to visit?

Why did he flee the place where
his only child was born? Did Clara
know he was not the sort of spouse
who would ever come home for dinner?

Was he playboy or monk?
Ariel or Prospero?
Why does he look like a man
holding a bouquet of roses behind his back?

We keep wondering about those eyes.
Is their expression wise or precious?
Or clever? Or is it condescending?
And what did he have against Christmas?

Only the poets love Rilke.
Others are perplexed—some men snicker
but women tend to smile as if waiting
for one flawless rose.

My students are desolate with questions.
Feminists bridle, the athletes stare.
We want to interview him there in his
abandoned garden house some Sunday afternoon.

Leda

Were you awake or asleep?

I was keeping my eyes open.
I was twisting my bone bracelet
and watching the bliss of a white petal
giving itself to the wind.

What was it that you wanted?

I wanted to enter a world without color,
a world where whiteness was everything.
I wanted the wind to give a definitive answer.

Whose life were you leading then?

My feelings were not my own.
I was leading the life of statues,
my body stony but penetrable.

How did the swan come to you?

It was April. The sun was
hidden behind a scrim of clouds.
I heard wind in the almond tree and turned.
There was no explicit shape.
There was a fire of white petals.
Then the spaces between things disappeared.

Was speech possible?

There were no edges. No words.
Something else took control. I felt
my eyes close, my chin brush my chest.
There were no words. Only breath and wings.

What is the last thing you remember?

I remember pain and beauty.
I remember the way feeling returned
like a formal accusation.

The Years with Bertran de Born

It took me years to understand I had been using
my head as a lantern like Dante's Bertran de Born,
I had been holding it carefully above my shoulders
as imagination led me out of sorrow
and darkness into meadows of light
but in photographs I was the one with my head
in my hands and black circles under my eyes,
the one meditating in Carthusian silence
though I broke it now and then with a whisper
or a moan and when there were gardens
they were always empty or if there were doors
they were always shut and maybe the sighing
of the wind was really the voice of a warrior
or a monk like Bertran de Born never knowing
when he woke each morning whether he would
murder or pray, he was the shameless devoted comrade
keeping medieval morality at bay for all of us,
lighting candle after candle at the tomb of the libido,
playing scenes dictated by dreams long ago,
there were decades of waiting at the outposts of lust
and years of lonely striving in the desert—
whole lifetimes spent on the battlefield
of our own crazed longings—we were the true
hostages of desire, Bertran and I, we would have
risked anything for each other in another life.

You Wake as the Charioteer of Delphi

With shards of dream threading the galactic breeze,
with a certain stutter in the air like the after-ring
of smoke, you know when you wake that you are
finally free and though you had once lived by craving,
though like a martyr you had picked up your head
and gone into a cave to hide, you are floating
in a pulsed stasis now, there is a low chiming
if you should try to blink and with your body
frozen into place, with your heart slowing down
so you can count the beats, you are sheathed and
    fluted
in a column of repose, there is a bell that rings
if you should try to raise your arm and block the sun
but this is not noon, this is the burning weight
of a new life—the click and whir of a key as it
turns inside the lock—and only when you try to breathe
do you begin to measure the distance you have come
which is why you lie down standing upright now
as if there were no end to this vigil of silence
while somewhere caryatids shiver and mountains
listen waist-deep in light as the long phantom
ride continues—this triumphant sway and lift
on the resounding paths of infinity.

A Studio in November

No sleep in the long wait for morning light.
No heat yet the sound of winter rain warms her.

She makes a mask of her face
and wears a paper dress imprinted with her name.

This is not Fiesole or Rome but the home
ghosts enter and leave through the floors or windows.

Is the body a mirror or a house?
Can she free herself from the bondage of images—

her own face covered with leaves,
the kore standing watch inside her soul.

All day she works behind a shuttered door
through which she drifts and quietly explodes.

What the Horses Know

The horses are roaming
the canyons dazed and
riderless they will not
wait for us because
we are always so far
behind it is hard to be
lost and lonely in these
dark valleys but the horses
know we will find them
by scent or by breath
there is enough pain left
in every nightfall to grip
the heart there is an after-ring
of anguish in every smile
and though we make promises
to each other with words
that do not belong to us
a silence will come
when we will know
what the horses know
hear the hooves
rumbling under bare
backlit shadows
gliding over the plain
feel the force of soul
in all that knows how
to move rhythmically
through the dark.

Rita Signorelli-Pappas' poems have been widely published in such journals as *Poetry, Shenandoah, Southwest Review, Prairie Schooner, The Literary Review, Poet Lore, The Women's Review of Books,* and *Southern Poetry Review,* and also in such online publications as *Poetry Daily* and *Verse Daily.* Her first poetry collection, *Satyr's Wife,* was published in 2010 by Serving House Books. It was favorably reviewed in *Italian Americana.* Her fiction has appeared in *Helicon Nine, Crosscurrents, Italian Americana, Farmer's Market, and VIA.* One of her short stories was nominated for a Pushcart Prize and another received the fiction award in *Italian Americana.*

Her other poetry activities include her having been a regular poetry reviewer for *World Literature Today* and having given a number of poetry readings at places like the (now defunct) Cornelia Street Café in New York City; Queensborough Community College in New York; Arcadia University, Valparaiso University; The Michigan City Public Library in Michigan City, Indiana; Barnes and Noble in Princeton, New Jersey; and The Writer's Room in Doylestown, Pennsylvania. She has also been a featured reader in the Poetry Night series at the Highland Park Public Library in New Jersey.

www.ingramcontent.com/pod-product-compliance
Lightning Source LLC
Chambersburg PA
CBHW020121130526
44591CB00031B/244